To - Pally

I hope you enjoy Ernest's trip
down memory lane. May you continue
on your journey of God's grace.
You are an inspiration to us all—

Love—
Martha

Growing Up on Grace

Ernest Spiva, Jr.

Wanda McGee
Editor
Ann Edmondson
Associate-Editor

Diana McQuagge
Business Manager

Illustrations by
Judy Broome-Riviere

Cover design by
Jason M. Heath

ISBN: 978-1-4834-4293-8 (sc)
ISBN: 978-1-4834-4292-1 (e)

Lulu Publishing Services rev. date: 12/22/2015

Contents

Foreword

Ernest was the descendant of two Bay County pioneer families–Stephen A. Spiva and William J. Harrison. As an entertaining storyteller, he enjoyed reminiscing about "the good old days." vividly recalled his own experiences as well as embellishing family tales. This book began from articles that he had written for several community anthologies. His first submission "Blow the Man Down" was about his grandfather and father who were early St. Andrew Bay harbor pilots. *Bay Lines* was funded by a grant to the Bay Humanities Council in 1981. In 2000 he wrote "Mama's Coming" about his maternal grandmother for *Pelican Tracks Vol 5* produced by the Panhandle Writers Guild. In preparation for the Panama City Centennial in 2009, current and former residents were encouraged to share their memories "in their own voice." *The Heritage of Bay County, Florida* was published in 2005. It was so successful that a Vol II was published in 2011. The story "Growing Up on Grace" was written for the first anthology and became the title for his book. In Vol II he expanded the stories and submitted "Ernest Spiva Remembers" When friends would drop by, he would regale them with stories and periodically would be inspired to record some of them in the yellow pad that he kept by his recliner. He reflected on the fun and adventures of growing up as well as the struggle of deciding what to do with his life. Ernest was influenced by such diverse adults as a local doctor, a band director, an aging Latin teacher, a funeral home director and an auto mechanic. His love of cars is evident throughout the book. After he retired, he wrote the book that ended with the graduation of the Rutherford Class of 1999. The book was not published in his lifetime. In loving memory, I have completed our story.

Martha

Dedication

Dedicated in honor of my wife Martha, who has inspired me
to do things that I would not have considered without her.

She "raised me up…"

Ernest Spiva, Jr.
March 2012

Martha Costin and Ernest Spiva, November 22, 1962.

Acknowledgements

The publication of this book would not have been possible without the contributions of others. I am especially indebted to the following people:

Wanda McGee for the editing, design, and layout of the book
Tony Simmons for the "Afterword" and providing editorial and technical
    assistance
Rachel Campbell for typing the original manuscript
Judy Broome-Riviere for the illustrations and "In Conclusion"
Beverly Fraser for "Reflections on a Collector"
Jason M. Heath, instructor of Digital Design at Haney Technical Center
Glenda Walters for content on the back cover
Mary Alma Hamlin, Yvette Herr, Marlene Womack and Faith Holman
    for proofreading

Picture credits:

Jennifer Fenwick-Photo collage
Ruth Glenn—Panama Grammar
Gayle Swatts—boating pictures
Steve Wilson—Bay County Elementary Band
Panama City News Herald
Bay County Library History & Genealogy Department
Bay District Schools Publications
Bay Medical Center Foundation—back cover

Ernest's book expresses gratitude for the people who influenced him on his life journey. He cherished his children and grandchildren, and appreciated friends, former students, teachers, parents, and colleagues.

Growing Up on Grace

Snow on Grace Avenue in the 1940s

After having been born at High Point on Williams Bayou and living all over the county (Washington County first, Bay County after 1913) my father chose to build the only house he ever built on Grace Avenue, at the corner of 10th Street in Panama City, Florida. In the early 1930's, his new house was built with cutting-edge materials, a large screened porch, indoor plumbing, a huge living room with a fireplace, and two large bedrooms. The refrigerator was on the back porch and was a Norge Electric. Getting a drink of milk at bedtime meant going outside.

"Sister" and Daddy admiring my first set of wheels

1

*Mother and me in
the front yard*

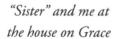 *"Sister" and me at
the house on Grace*

With Charles McGill, my earliest neighborhood friend

My first dog, Mutt

My sister, Betty Sue, had her own bedroom, and enjoyed living in the new house, close to everything. When I came along in 1937, another bedroom was added—complete with fuel-oil heater to allow for the retirement of the fireplace.

Grace Avenue, named for the granddaughter of a pioneer settler, was the site of many grand homes of early community leaders, but it was considered "out in the country." and the pavement ended at 11th Street, which was also just a dirt road. We had a close-knit neighborhood, and I still have contact with some of our Grace Avenue friends to this day.

We had all the infrastructure of a modern city: water, sewer (which was dumped raw into the bay at the foot of Harrison Avenue), dependable electricity, and telephones with consecutively assigned numbers— ours was number 223. My friends, the McGills, had number 598. You picked up the old, heavy black phone in the living room and heard, "Number, please," and the operator rang your party for you. We had a grocery store or two, schools, our church, the Gulf station, and all the Harrison Avenue businesses—all

My first graduation (kindergarten)

within walking distance. Families usually had just one car.

Panama Grammar School served our community in the building formerly housing the high school, which moved north on Harrison Avenue to its present location in 1926. The Bay High "Alma Mater" begins with "On our city's northern border"!!!

Principal Hugh Brock in front of Panama Grammar

Students on the fire escape of Panama Grammar

School Days 1951-52
Jinks Junior High

We walked to Panama Grammar for grades 1 through 8, after attending Mrs. Forman's Kindergarten in the 700 block of Grace Avenue.

There were no buses and only a few teachers had cars. It was very easy for teachers to send a note home to your parents at lunch to be signed and returned that afternoon.

I could hear playground noises at my house, and even the single outside bell could be heard at my house.

During the war (WWII), our Grace Avenue Block Warden was our neighbor, Mr. Bill Weaver, who happened to be principal at Bay County High School. Mrs. Weaver taught at Panama Grammar. Today, the old Panama Grammar building is the educational building for the First Presbyterian Church.

Fifteenth birthday with twins Mack and Sam
Carmichael at the house on Grace

During air raid drills, a huge siren on a telephone pole nearby would signal us to pull all the shades and darken the houses. Mr. Weaver would appear in his helmet and armband and check the neighborhood for any signs of light coming from the houses.

Cars had their headlights partially blacked out and streetlights along the bay had their waterfront half blacked out. Pretty scary reminders of wartime for all us kids!

Out in the "sure nuff" woods on 11th street, a new school was begun when I was in the 7th grade. It was called Jinks Junior High School and would house grades 7, 8, and 9. As often happens, construction was not completed in time for school's opening, so the old, wartime housing complex, Annie B. Sale Project, was used for a year to house Jinks Junior High—*ad interim* the sign said. Tommy Oliver Stadium is located on the site today.

My 8th grade year was spent in an old government apartment, with walls removed and the holes for plumbing closed up with tin nailed over them.

But what a great year it was, thanks to our wonderful teacher, Miss Vivian Brady! She made our 13th year of life a happy, positive, quickly-passing one!

We moved into our new school on still-to-be-paved 11th street for the 9th grade, and were met with buses, a cafeteria, showers, football team, and marching band. We *ran off* the yearbook in green ink all by ourselves. Why, we even had automatic bells and a school-wide PA system!

We also had something new, called an "assistant principal." But that's a whole 'nother story. Let me just say that I could still walk home with a message for my parents in no time at all.

Bay High's band director, Mr. Orin Whitley, also taught our band class. He lived in our neighborhood, and had a huge German shepherd named Major.

Bay County Elementary Band in the late 1940s

Mr. Whitley came over from the high school and daily revealed to us an exciting peek at glorious things to come—our high school days at Bay County High School.

"On our city's northern border" didn't quite fit Bay High when we arrived for our first year there, our sophomore year. We still had to walk to school. Riding bikes was uncool, and few 10th graders could drive. Soooo, it was, "Walk yourself those two blocks, boy!"

For the first time, Grace Avenue wasn't so great. Why couldn't we live in Southport or somewhere so I could ride the bus? High school days soon passed into the "years rolled by" as the "Alma Mater" predicted. And when I would come home from college, and later from the U.S. Army, I sometimes would bring friends for a visit. I would drive downtown on Grace Avenue and point out where the mayor lived and the first swimming pool to be built there. I would point out my preacher's house, my doctor's house, several teachers' houses, the judge's house, and countless houses occupied by friends and classmates, long since gone now.

The once-new sidewalk, where we skated with our metal skates, clamped on to our shoes by a key, is cracked and patched now. But it ran in front of everybody's house, and it hooked us all together, so I would point it out, too. It was important.

Finally, I would show my guests the First Baptist Church and tell about riding my tricycle to Sunday school, before I was big enough to tackle riding a bicycle!

Grace Avenue is still there. A few old-timers are still there. But my memories of our "place on Grace" will never go away.

How lucky we were!

Bay High graduation.
May 30th, 1955

"Blow the Man Down"

Daddy and me on the steps at Grace Avenue

That old sea chantey haunts my memory! My father used to sing that to me as his father sang it to him. They both were Harbor Pilots or, more correctly, Bar Pilots, who are trained to guide vessels into and out of specific ports. They dock and undock the large ships and are legally responsible for the movement of the vessels until they are out to sea again. A "pilot boat" meets the large vessel out in the sea-lanes and "puts the pilot aboard" the ship, with the pilot climbing a ladder up the side of the ship. During this time, the boatman must keep the pilot boat hard against the larger vessel to allow for a margin of safety. The reverse procedure takes place when a ship leaves port. Physical conditioning is very important to prevent serious accidents. Knowledge of the port and the handling of large ships come only after years of practice and study.

While the Civil War was still loud in their ears and its memories were still strong in the hearts of St. Andrews Bay citizens, my great-grandfather, Stephen Augustus Spiva, moved his family from Kentucky to the St. Andrews area, during the "Cincinnati Boom" which brought Yankees to St. Andrews Bay.

Being a former Union soldier probably had some bearing on his trek to northwest Florida, and perhaps he came to try to find his long-lost brother who had fought for the Confederacy and was not seen again. Luckily for all his descendants, he did come to this place we love so much! A millwright, he set up a sawmill in St. Andrews in 1886, but was not to achieve success in this venture.

Stephen Augustus Spiva moved his family to the High Point area, where he "proved up" a homestead. One of his seven sons, William Eldridge Spiva, my grandfather, was in his late teens at this time. Stephen A. Spiva died in 1887, and was buried with his sister, Mollie, and an infant in the family cemetery on the homestead. All were later moved by my father to the family plot in Greenwood Cemetery.

The original Pilot boat

William Eldridge Spiva, while helping clear and further establish the Spiva homestead on what was North Bay, married my grandmother, Mary Olivia (Mollie) Brown, in 1886. She was from Econfina, Florida, and her father was Benjamin Bartlett Brown, who served in Company K, 6th Florida Infantry and CSA (Confederate States of America).

After just a few years, William E. Spiva became "Captain Spiva" of the St. Andrews Bay Pilots' Association in 1908. Earlier pilots for the port city of St. Andrews were Captain A. Alexander and T.L. Croft.

These, along with my grandfather, were listed on the company letterhead, in 1917, which proudly boasted of the location of the pilot station as Hurricane Island. The pilot station was destroyed by a hurricane in 1927

Many other pilots have since come and gone, and their memory lingers in our area's history.

Pilot boat, Capt. W.E. Spiva, named after my grandfather

Cost of doing business in 1917

William E. Spiva's pilot's license, 1930

Captain W. E. Spiva served as a bar pilot until his death in 1933, a period of some twenty-five years. He carried on the tradition of the sea that had become a way of life for this Kentucky family.

In 1904, my father, Ernest Raymond Spiva, was born at the homestead on Williams Bayou, just above the present-day Deer Point Dam. The family was soon moved to Millville, by Captain W. E. Spiva, to be nearer his work at piloting. Later, they made their last move back to St. Andrews on the bay. It was during this period that my father would walk down the beach with his father on the way to or from Panama City or Millville. The only road at that time was near today's 15th Street! These long walks gave father and son precious hours together, part of which were spent singing and "spinning yarns" which both liked to do.

Portrait of Captain W.E. Spiva and wife, Mollie, with their
daughter, Willie, and son, Ernest (circa 1914 by E.W. Masker)

Mama's Coming

Mother and Mama in our living room at
1005 Grace Avenue (circa 1940)

In my family, the name "Mama" was reserved for only one person. There was "Mother," "Mom," "Grandmother," but only one Mama—my grandmother, Mrs. Seaborn Lisenby, Aunt Purlieu, Mrs. W.J. Harrison, Purlieu Alexander, or "Mama."

She was my mother's mother. Born in Henry County, Alabama, she barely missed the agony of the Civil War. She lived her prime years during the Reconstruction and the beginning of the "New Century." The Yankees were still not to be trusted, and besides, who knew what those Catholics might be hiding in their basements!

Born Martha Elizabeth Purlieu Marilda Alexander, Purlieu was the name the family most often used.

Mama married William Jeremiah Harrison. They lived in Greenwood, just above Marianna, where my mother was born. Papa Harrison had sawmills: one in Greenwood and one in Lynn Haven.

The Harrison family spent summers in Lynn Haven and enjoyed the wonderful life the area afforded year around. Life-long friendships were formed. The Harrison children all began families of their own, who, for the most part, remained in the area.

Mama was a devout, God-fearing Baptist. Her brother, Coleman Alexander, was a Baptist minister. The church and all its facets were part of Mama's fabric and dictated her path each day.

In the midst of "the good old days," Papa Harrison got sick and died. Mama's journal, a daily diary, was written in a U.S. Department of Commerce, leather-bound, "Light Station Journal," and it tells a profound, proud history of Mama's daily life from 1918 until

Mama dressed for church

1935, when it just stops, with many blank pages left in the bound journal.

On the day her husband died, in 1925, Mama wrote, "…Jeremiah was called away at 11:00 a.m., April 1ˢᵗ. They embalmed him that day and prepared him for burial with the Masons acting as pallbearers…about sun down…"

The next entry was a few days later, on April 11ᵗʰ, when she wrote, "Elaine went to Mobile to a party today. She had a good time."

Form 801
Department of Commerce and Labor
LIGHTHOUSE SERVICE

JOURNAL of Light Station at *fet the 1st 1925*

19 MONTH	DAY.	STATE WORK PERFORMED BY KEEPERS REGARDING UPKEEP OF STATION, AND RECORD OF IMPORTANT EVENTS, BAD WEATHER, ETC.
Feb	1st	moved to the county bridge
"	2	Florine commenced to board at mr Riley
"	7	Robbert came & stayed till the 8th
Mch	19	Jeremiah was taken bad off sick with a pain in his left side. We called Dr Whitfield & Dr Lowe They both came & examined him & consulted pronounced the pain gas. Sat the 21 he had a bad stroke in his left side never could sit up any more nor could talk but to whisper a little. On april the 1st it being wednesday he was called away at 11 a.m. They embalmed him on the 1st & prepared for burial They nd we had his funeral at the baptist church the masons acting as pall bearers After the funeral we took him to Dothan got there & buried him bout sundown The masons performed their ceremony & had prayer

A page from Mama's journal describing Papa Harrison's passing

In Mama's journal, which is our most-treasured family heirloom, she recorded forever the daily activities deemed important to a 1918 to 1935-era housewife and mother.

Mama described which row was planted with the most exotic species of cabbage seed, and how very special the new 1925 Star automobile was to the family.

Mama with first husband W. J. Harrison, and oldest child Lillie Maude (circa 1915)

Chronicled each day was the weather, who visited whom, who died, who was sick, and which doctors came on the weekend, making their rounds.

Recipes for special home remedies were sprinkled throughout the journal, some on yellow newspaper pages from *Circle Magazine* and others.

Ailments and afflictions, long-since conquered, were sadly discussed, and lengthy hospital stays were the norm. Taking the heater down in April and the approach of the "September storm" were deemed annual milestones.

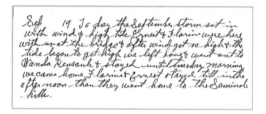

Description of 1926 September storm

The purchase of the family cow is mentioned, as are the prices of groceries, seeds, and plants.

Mama, Papa Harrison, and their youngest child, Wallace, moved to the "county bridge" crossing North Bay, shortly before Papa died. Mama and Wallace served as bridge tenders after his death. Mama was Mrs. W. J. Harrison, and she took charge of the family.

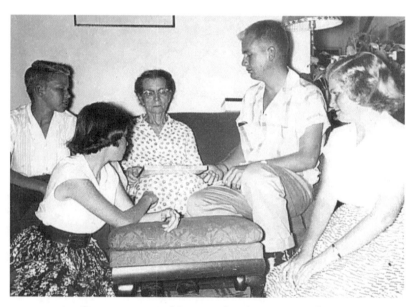

Cousins visiting Mama at her house in Dothan

Mama and her children in Dothan: (from left) Mildred (Wallace's wife),
Mother (Florine), Elaine, Mama, Wallace, and Floyd

Elaine, Mama, and
Mother (Florine)
ready for an outing
in "Panama"

When all her children had children, we "cousins" visited Mama's big house on south St. Andrew Street in Dothan. Johnny Mack Brown, of western fame, lived across the street. Mama's house was large enough for each family to have their own bedrooms during visits. Well do I remember the lengthy blessing offered by Seaborn Lisenby, who was the retired Dothan postmaster. When we went to visit Mama, her children—Wallace Harrison, Elaine Harrison Wiselogel, Floyd Harrison Campbell, and Florine Harrison Spiva—would bring their children and fill the big house.

When Mama would visit Panama, not Panama City but "Panama," the children would vie to be her host or hostess.

In 1963, Mama, too, was called away. We all went to Dothan and buried her—about sunset. She rests today beside William Jeremiah Harrison, her first husband and father of her children. Not far away, lies her sister Mallie Alexander and her second husband, Seaborn Lisenby—still near each other in that old, beautiful cemetery.

But Can We Still Play War?

I was just eight years old and the radio said that World War II was over. I didn't remember anything before the war. I didn't even know when the war started.

We lived near downtown Panama City, and later-to-be Mayor Frank Nelson loaded all of us in the car and drove all over town with horns blasting, lights flashing, and the town's sirens wailing! Absolute pandemonium in the streets! **The War was over!**

Several times, one of us asked Frank, "Can we still play war now?" Wisely, he said each time, "If you want to, you sure can."

My very first memory of any "war stuff" was in my own house. Way down south in Panama City on Grace Avenue, a block before the pavement ended. Safe at home with Mother and Daddy. But the specter of war lurked in the background.

Daddy, like his father, was a harbor pilot, a bar pilot. No ships could come into St. Andrews Bay without having a bar pilot come out into the Gulf and climb up a rope ladder onto the ship and guide or "pilot" the ship to the dock.

But we were at war, and the Gulf was not really safe, especially at night. Ships had been sunk. Periscopes had been sighted.

Our telephone at home was Daddy's link with that terrifying, nebulous presence: the enemy, the 'Japs', and the Germans.

When the operator rang our number, 223, that ancient black telephone's wall-mounted bells signaled an alert. When I answered and the caller asked for "Captain Spiva," I knew to leave the room, but nobody could stop me from listening.

Gas rationing cards and mileage supplement.

Shipping schedules were secret, and codes were used on the telephone in whispered references to things like cups, saucers, and plates. The federalized business of wartime shipping took place in our house with the rose bushes and the playhouse for my sister.

We had to put black-out shades on every window and practice "air raid warnings." No visible lights. Even the streetlights had covers on them to make them invisible from above.

No waterfront lights were allowed. The street lamps had their waterfront sides painted black, and car headlights were painted black on the top half. No fires were allowed on the beaches. A single cigarette was visible from an airplane!

Air raid wardens patrolled their blocks, complete with helmet, armbands, whistle, and flashlight. Ours was Bay County High School principal, Bill Weaver.

He walked his post up and down the street, giving all residents a critique on our black-out efforts. He would stop by each front porch and chat with all of us. The "all clear" siren would end the drill, and we were thankful that all these events were, in fact, drills.

The town siren was a huge contraption on top of the city hall-jail-police station and fire station. It sounded a code for the ward in which the fire was located. For air raid drills, there were auxiliary sirens located around town. Ours was on a telephone pole, and I was afraid of those constant war reminders, even when they were just silently lurking.

Rationing of food and gasoline was regulated by the Office of Price Administration. Stamps and coupons were needed, along with the money, and cars had a gas-rationing sticker. Daddy had a "C" sticker because of his need to get to the pilot boat often.

The pilot boat was painted black and used no running lights as it took the pilot out in the Gulf to get on a ship, or as it took the pilot off the ship after it left safe port.

There were no radios on the pilot boat, and I remember Daddy studying Morse code for some reason.

At night, the bay was frequently full of all sorts of ships, seeking safety from U-Boats. There were two-gun emplacements at the jetties, and a small artillery detachment was quartered nearby.

I remember the bay full of huge landing ships at anchor all along Beach Drive, and Daddy and the three other pilots wearily meeting in the kitchen, planning on how to get the landing ship through the pass at first light.

This dangerous lifestyle took its toll on my parents, and they died earlier than many of their contemporaries. Never did they tell us that the next trip "down the bay," as it was termed, would possibly be the last for my daddy.

When I talked about being a pilot someday, I was always encouraged to do something safe. Something else!

Daddy would bring home gifts from the Navy ship captains, tell of beautiful Gulf waters, and sometimes he came home with a few spent shells from artillery practice at the jetties. What a life, I thought!

We listened to WDLP all the time. Radios were placed in windows, and you could hear them all over the neighborhood. When Gabriel Heater came on at 8:00 p.m., we knew it was time to go inside.

We all participated in the war effort. We saved fats and grease for the Girl Scouts and their salvage drives. Smack in the middle of Harrison Avenue and 4th Street was a large pen for holding old pots and pans for scrap metal. I loved to miss the pen and hear Daddy "cuss" when he had to stop traffic to retrieve a skillet!

Nothing brought our country together as did the war. *Victory Gardens*, scrap metal drives, and rationing of essentials for the troops—all helped foster a community unity attitude that I'll never forget.

"Sister" driving the 1941 Chevy that carried us through the war

We even rented our front bedroom on Grace Avenue to soldiers stationed at Tyndall Field Army Air Corps Base. My sister met her future husband, Dan, when he joined hundreds of young Americans stationed at bustling Tyndall Field.

The war brought us together and made us closer just as fear always does. The newsreels at the weekly Ritz Theater Kiddee Matinee kept us focused on the war. The Saturday westerns and "serials" were the center of our lives, but we watched the newsreels, too.

When the war was over, I know we filled some adults with consternation as we asked in youthful innocence, ". . . but, can we still play war?"

"Sister" and her future husband, Dan Kimmel

The Camping Bug

In the 1940's, Crosley made a new refrigerator with shelves in the door. The "Shelvador" was a best seller, and the Furniture Mart on Harrison Avenue sold them fast.

Yeah, my parents bought a Shelvador and even the matching radio to sit on top. But what is important for you to know about is the box the fridges came in.

These boxes were cardboard with wooden reinforcing, and the bottoms were cut off to allow the box to be lifted free of the Shelvador.

They made perfect "campers." We all had our Radio Flyer wagons, and a Shelvador box could be tied on with the opening facing the rear. A towel made a door, and we learned the best way to cut little window flaps. For waterproofing, a coat of paint made the cardboard water repellent. Best of all, you could trade in your old camper when somebody bought a new Shelvador! Every boy in the neighborhood checked the trash bin at the Furniture Mart on a regular basis!

These campers were light and sturdy and easy to pull. There was plenty of room for one little boy and all his stuff. They were very cozy on a cold winter day when the window flaps were closed.

We ranged about two miles from home, at the most, and I particularly remember our favorite spot being across Beach Drive from the Bayside Inn on Johnson Bayou.

A bunch of painted boxes on wagons parked together by a group of tow-headed kids! Great memories.

First trip in our first real camper, at St. Joseph State Park,
with visiting Port St. Joe relatives (circa 1970)

We soon got too "cool" for wagons and Shelvador boxes. But we all agreed that there was nothing to supplant them. I missed my camper.

About fifteen or sixteen years later, my wife, Martha, and I bought an old, slide-in camper for a short-bed pickup for $500.00. I had to borrow a truck to even get the camper home!

Soon, we had the camper tied on the back of an old Ford truck and, with my young family, Gary, Lee, and Susan, diapers and all; we lit out for the mountains and adventures that are still unfolding.

Here we go again!

The kids are grown now, but they still go with us to our beloved mountains, from time to time. It's usually just Martha and me, in our rather huge box on wheels with room for our stuff. We go thousands of miles from home now.

When I'm asked by my friends why I like to drive a huge box to far-away places, and then go through the rigors of setting up and living with miniscule appliances and primitive accommodations, I just say, "You might not understand. It's a Shelvador Thing!"

Water to Swim in, to Fish in, to Look at

When my parents would reminisce, they would talk about how the land on Grace Avenue sloped down to the bay before the buildings and trees blocked the view.

They would remark that the cool, southeast breeze that we enjoyed blew from that bay.

But, in my earliest memory, the bay was polluted with sewage from the waterfront homes and the city sewers, which discharged from the seawall at the foot of Harrison Avenue.

Soooo, we couldn't swim or fish close to town in our beautiful bay, not until I was eight or nine, anyway.

When I took swimming lessons, about the 1st grade or so, we went to Lynn Haven, where I was taught by an old man who had had a stroke. The water in North Bay was cleaner, I suppose.

My earliest memory of "swimming" was in the Gulf and in Lake Merial and White Western Lake, the two closest Sand Hill ponds to town. Fresh water swimming was very special, but we had to drive to Sand Hill Ponds on dirt roads, and we never went often enough. My mother always took me and some friends to the ponds. I remember well how skillfully she drove the big old Dodge family sedan down the sandy, rut roads and across the occasional washout that sometimes appeared in the "wet season."

She insisted that I learn the backstroke, and the still, clear waters of the ponds were the ideal place for backstroking. She was quite an athlete.

In my elementary school days, Mr. Travis Childs, owner of Walgreen's, had built the first local swimming pool half a block away in the 900 block of Grace Avenue.

Giving Little Nancy a ride on my scooter
around the neighborhood

We got to swim there some, and I took the Red Cross lifesaving course just to get in that pool. Today, the pool is filled in with a concrete parking lot!

In junior high, I learned about Bear Creek and Indian Bluff Resort. High diving into the cold, dark creek from huge diving platforms was the mark of "being a man," and it was the goal of all of us to "go off the top board"—sooner or later.

Indian Bluff was almost an hour's drive down a dirt road, far away. We didn't go there often!

Much closer was Mill Bayou Creek, complete with a railroad trestle. We swam on the south side of Highway 231, around a corner, just past the trestle. It was the closest fresh water to Grace Avenue!

The only times I went there were on my Sears Allstate Motor Scooter, which I had from fourteen to sixteen years of age. I parked the scooter under the highway bridge because I wasn't sure I was allowed to go that far on my scooter. I don't think I ever talked about Mill Bayou to my parents!

My boundaries on the scooter were simply, "the two bay bridges." We lived on the bay, for about a year when I was four or five, in my grandmother's house in St. Andrews. Mother and Daddy bought a house on Bunker's Cove, where we lived until I finished kindergarten.

In the Cove, I was forbidden to swim there because of the pollution. There wasn't even a path to the beach. We just had a steep trail down to the dock and a spectacular view. Beautiful sunsets! Then Grace Avenue called us, and we moved back home to the house Daddy built.

My teenage years were spent on the now-clean waters of the "Little Bay," between Redfish Point and Freshwater Bayou. We did go into Watson Bayou and Massalina Bayou, but we stayed mainly in front of the Yacht Club in our sailboats.

A good friend got a boat for her birthday, and we would make the sometimes treacherous voyage from Lake Caroline to the Yacht Club, across the always-rough bay front near the Standard Oil dock.

We couldn't drive legally on the roads, but her boat opened the door for our bunch to get out on the water. We also water-skied behind that boat, and we were small enough to be snatched right along by the 15-horse Evinrude!

When the tide was out, we had problems getting home to Lake Caroline and power tilt was just a dream, as was an electric hoist for the boathouse!

After the sewer system cleaned things up, we crabbed, scalloped, and caught oysters along the shorelines.

Going to the Saint Andrew Bay Yacht Cub with the Seymour brothers

33

I would walk on St. Andrews and Lynn Haven beaches with an oyster knife and a bottle of Tabasco sauce, and eat my fill of oysters with no worries.

I never learned how to clean blue crabs because we were taught to break off only the one pincher and throw the crab back. Nobody ate the whole crab! Docks and bridges were places to catch fish and crabs. We found that you could eat chofers and hardtails if you prepared them right. But mostly, we used our catches to fertilize the rose bushes.

In front of Saint Andrew Bay Yacht Club in our sailboats

Much of the waterfront hasn't changed and my memories are centered around the bay. I can still go look at my childhood playground today. Thank you, Lord!

Nowadays, all I have to do is catch a whiff of the smells associated with the water: low tide, the paper mill, piney sand hill woods—and it all comes back.

Just to look at it is enough now. I never realized that "getting to the water" in my youth would generate so many golden thoughts for today. How lucky we were!

Orin Whitley

Mr. Whitley chaperoning the band bus

Outside my family, there was certainly no more profound influence on my formative years than Mr. Orin Whitley.

He lived a block north, on Jenks Avenue, and he frequently walked his huge dog past our house. He also shopped at Tip Top Grocery and was well known in our neighborhood, along with his wife, Betty, and his daughter, Sherry.

Mr. Whitley was the Bay County High School band director. He came to the school in 1938, after graduating from the University of Florida with a degree in music.

I guess he was considered the "head director" of all county schools since the elementary schools all fed into Bay High. When junior highs were started here in 1950, Jinks and Everitt became the only Bay feeder schools.

Maybe he knew about the coming junior highs and their marching bands and athletic programs, because Mr. Whitley put on a recruitment program at Panama Grammar School (and others, too, I suppose) for new 5th graders.

We all got together in the auditorium to hear and see Mr. Whitley and a group of band members demonstrate various instruments. It was sort of intimidating. I was barely ten years old. My parents made all of my big decisions, and here we were about to make a life-changing decision. And I do mean for the rest of my life.

We met in a building where the band practiced, as directed by Mr. Whitley, if we were interested in playing an instrument. He went around the dozen or so kids saying "trumpet, trombone, clarinet," and we were thus *chosen* for our major pursuit for the coming years. Mr. Whitley chastised one of my friends for talking, and he never returned to be a band member. It was my friend's loss!

We didn't know it, but our decision had far more impact on us than just a few music skills and learning to march and play.

We had our own band teacher in the 5th, 6th, and 7th grades at Panama Grammar, and we had concerts and even played for the 8th grade graduation. "Pomp and Circumstance" at Panama Grammar!

In junior high, our band director was unable to control the band properly, and after one year, Mr. Whitley came over for our band class. As 9th graders, we were expected to be seated and ready to play for Mr. Whitley. If he was late, we managed to play with student leaders.

He was particularly upset with me one day as he arrived. He grabbed me by the collar and lifted me out of my chair as he told me what he would beat out of me next time. There was no "next time." Mr. Whitley became the most respected teacher I had at Jinks that year, and I faced three years of high school with him!

We wore white shirts and pants and played at Bay High's graduation (class of 1952) with the Everitt Junior High kids. They also had white shirts and pants—thanks to the vision,

Bay High band uniforms in 1955

planning, and influence of Orin Whitley.

Even though he yelled and cajoled, it was fun! We were good. We were scared not to be. He used phrases and "descriptives" like no other! He would say, after we loused something up, "Don't use main strength and awkwardness in here. Use skill."

In high school, band practice was held two nights a week. A new halftime show was performed every week at a football game—new music to be memorized, new routines. Band classes for five days and two night rehearsals—and then Friday night! His halftime shows were legendary. He used all sorts of gadgets and loved to turn off the field lights and do shows in the dark! He used excerpts from classic pieces, such as "In the Hall of the Mountain King," from Grieg's *Pier Gynt Suite*, to introduce us to the world of classical music. But we played this stuff from memory, out on the field, marching in the dark, with his lights on our feet!

And those lights flashed on and off when you took a step. No way could you cover up being out of step! And Orin Whitley invented the lights and had them made in a local machine shop. The same shop that fixed my motor scooter!

The whole town would turn out for our practices, and we had Tommy Oliver Stadium to ourselves two nights per week. We even broadcasted radio programs live from the band room.

Built in 1947, the music building was designed by Mr. Whitley himself. It was modern, had gas heat, and featured fan-forced ventilation. Mr. Whitley once showed me his home's whole-house attic fan ventilator, which he built and installed.

Sue Perry and me outside the band bus

The music building had many individual practice rooms and was a showplace for band and choir programs. It was later named for Orin Whitley, in the early 1960s. The new music building at Bay High also bears his name.

There were many times that we didn't play at all. We would get out our horns and stuff and be seated, and for whatever reason, he would lecture us on a variety of subjects. And total silence reigned as he spoke about life, about loyalty, about honor, about honesty, about doing the right thing, and about taking care of each other. And about how he was always watching us!

No other teacher ever cared as much about us. What a great motivator! I wasn't sure if he trusted me to ever grow up or be dependable. After all, I did get a group of boys to "duck" him at a swimming party. (He took us all to the bottom and nearly drowned all of us!) When we were all coughing and sputtering, he laughed and said, "Anybody else?" There was none.

At graduation of the class of '54, in the gym, the band, once again in white shirts and pants, sat for hours as the names were called. I had smuggled in a thermos of cold grape juice, along with my music folder. I had a few paper cups, which I passed around with juice. One cup came back with a note in it saying, "I hope you have another cup. OW."

I passed a full cup to him, across the floor. I couldn't see him drink it. He never said a word, but I sure thought about it. Still do!

He had a 1950 Oldsmobile. It would outrun anything, we thought. One day after practice at the new Tommy Oliver Stadium, he gruffly told me to stay by his car. I was certain that death followed, but he threw me the keys, which I dropped, and said to drive his car to the band room for him. No threats, no direction. Trust.

I graduated shortly after that and the band, decked out in white with the Jinks and Everitt kids, played Mr. Whitley's last performance of "Pomp and Circumstance." I was shocked at my own emotion that night. I was not happy at graduation! Even Bay County School Superintendent Tommy Smith asked me when he handed me my diploma if I was going to make it.

After the class of '55 departed, one hot summer day, my mother woke me up early. She said that Mr. Whitley had died after a heart attack. He was forty-four years old! I have not gotten over that yet.

I went to the band room, climbed in an office window as I had done before, and opened the doors. Soon the place was full of "Million Dollar Band" alumni all the way back to the 1930s. Word was quickly passed around town. The camaraderie was what we needed, and the band room was where we had it taught to us. The profound sense of loss, surrounded by others with the same loss, and our utter devastation was almost unbearable.

The First Baptist Church was packed, and the funeral procession to Tallahassee set a record for length. On the way home, we tried to act our usual selves and be happy, but it was hard.

Colonel Bachman, director of the University of Florida Band, told me, at my audition, that it was my duty to Orin Whitley to be in the Gator Band, so I did it. But it wasn't the same.

When I transferred to FSU, each time Bay High's band passed through Tallahassee, the new director, Mr. Anthony McCarthy, would send me a telegram, inviting me to meet them. I never missed a time. It was the least I could do.

Bay County School Superintendent, Tommy Smith

Today, I am over a quarter century older than Orin Whitley was when he died. His teachings and his exacting demands taught me much. I will continue to use what he taught all of us until my last day.

I never took a formal class in music after my Bay High days, but seven years under Orin Whitley provided me with a lifetime supply of skills beyond the bass and the treble clef. Thanks, Mr. Whitley. What a treasure you were for hundreds of young citizens, all practicing being young adults. We didn't really know what we had in you.

But now...we know. And we are eternally grateful.

Ray Southerland

I first met Ray when I was just a little kid and he worked for Mr. Wilson. My sister was Betty Jean Wilson's best friend, and Betty lived upstairs at the Wilson Funeral Home.

Ray Southerland

When Ray opened up the funeral home on Harrison Avenue, I was leaving soon to go to college to major in medicine, and I was having the first huge crisis of my life, deciding just what to do in the future.

Ray became the most important influence on me, outside of my immediate family. My formative years were directed by the influence of Orin Whitley and now, by Ray Southerland.

He told me all about New Bern, North Carolina and his proud service in the Seabees in the "Big War." He talked about his old boss at Wilson's and revered him highly.

We spent many hours on seemingly impossible tasks at the funeral home. And he taught, and I listened and learned. He taught by precept and example, not words alone.

In addition to technical, biological, and professional skills, Ray gave personal, spiritual, and social directions as a part of my association with him.

I couldn't wait to become a Freemason and join St. Andrews Lodge with Ray and Steve, where I was inducted by my father, as he was by his father—but Ray was always there.

The Southerland family: Steve with wife, Mary Sue, Ray, and Bobbie

The Southerland family presented me with a Masonic Bible, a rite usually reserved for the family. But Ray, his wife Bobbie, and son Steve insisted on presenting that beautiful Masonic Bible to me.

When my first child was born, it was Ray and Bobbie who presented him with a savings bond for college.

You can't be around someone for very long without getting to know him or her pretty well. Any successes I may have had in life were surely a direct result of Ray's positive influence.

He taught me coolness in crises, how to keep your emotions from adversely affecting decisions, to always be dignified in your appearance, how to improvise, how to "do it yourself," and how to always respect your family. "God's watching you, son," he would say.

He even offered me a chance to come into the funeral profession when all my plans for the future seemed to change to pure uncertainty and bleakness. My anchor in the storm!

I will forever remember his voice when I called 785-8532 and he answered in his wonderful southern voice, "Southerland Funeral Home, Ray Southerland speaking."

God sent Ray to us. Ray's profound influence goes far, far, far, beyond his wonderful, loving family. And we are forever grateful.

The Masonic funeral ending perhaps says my feelings best: "…farewell, Brother Ray…"

Hathaway Bridge

Until 1928, travel to our Gulf beaches was chiefly by boat—because the so-called "roads" were merely sand trails from the North in Alabama. Why would anyone want to go to the beach?

Nothing would grow in the sand, and fresh water was not easily found. It was better to just sail by the beaches and travel on to Ft. Walton, Pensacola, and Mobile on motorized boats, such as the Tarpon.

The Gulf Coast Highway, today's U.S. 98, was completed with the opening of two identical bridges, DuPont and Hathaway, in 1928, smack in the heyday of the Ford Model T.

These two-lane, steel and concrete bridges brought Bay County into the modern era in North Florida.

The 1928 Hathaway Bridge viewed from the new 1959 bridge

The Intracoastal Waterway is a barge traffic highway passing through St. Andrews Bay, and these new bridges were too low to allow some barges to pass underneath. Thus, came the "draw bridge era" from 1928-1959. The center draw span sat on a pier, with the bridge tender's house located high over the roadway among the steel girders supporting the bridge.

When a barge or other craft approached Highway 98, the captain blew his whistle to signal the bridge tender to open the bridge. Both bridges are situated such that long-distance views are poor. Many times, the bridge tender didn't see or hear the approaching craft until almost too late!

Because of this geographic boondoggle, the drawbridge mechanism had to work pretty quickly. The gates were lowered, lights flashed up and down the bridge, and the draw was opened.

First, the locking arms were retracted just like opening the deadbolt on a door. The electric motor turned huge gears, and the entire span swung out to a 90-degree position.

At first, the gates were located at the edge of the draw span, but a few years later, they were moved back to allow a margin of safety if someone didn't stop in time!

I remember a taxicab going through the gate and sailing out into the open span, killing the driver!

When the boats or a long line of barges passed, the captain signaled the bridge tender with a single blast on the whistle, and closing began.

When the span returned to its closed position, those infernal, cantankerous locking arms had to be precisely engaged to support road traffic. Sometimes, it took a while. It was like trying to thread four needles with your arms fully outstretched.

And we all sat on the bridge, amid flashing lights and clanging bells, and waited. And waited! U.S. 98 was dead stopped. For thirty years! Until 1959.

Sometimes we all got out and socialized, and, yes, a few impatient souls turned around and drove back off the bridge to wait for another day.

Particularly exciting was driving an ambulance across the bridge in heavy traffic. Traffic would usually pull to the right and stop, but the ambulance could not pass unless the oncoming lane was clear. We finally discovered that the safest way to get across the bridge in an emergency was to turn off the red lights and siren and drive normally across, and then resume the Code Red on the other side. (Ray Southerland's sage instructions!)

Waiting on the bridge with a critically ill patient in the ambulance was a dreaded event!

In 1955, during my "senior celebration" in Bay High School, a carload of us was stopped forever on that bridge when we saw one of our teachers stopped behind us, too. She had a dentist's appointment and was missing the morning class, just like we were! We were toast! Thanks to that darn bridge!

The 1959 bridge's draw less span arrives, raised
high in order to be lowered in place

In 1959, the old bridges were replaced with a new, four-lane high-rise span. During this time I was employed by the Florida State Road Department and took a picture of the old bridge from the new one.

From the Model T's to the huge, finned behemoths of the '50s, the Hathaway Bridge served us well. Now, we are driving over a modern six-lane replacement.

Present day Hathaway Bridge

The Car Connection

Well, why not? I rode in a car with my parents to the place where I was born, and the doctor and nurse came in a car. After I was born, I even rode home in a car.

So cars are a major influence in my life. The first car I can remember was a new, pre-war 1940 Chevrolet four-door sedan, which was delivered by my uncle, Karl Wiselogel, who worked at Nelson Chevrolet.

The car had tags hanging from the cigar lighter (which glowed green when it was ready), the radio, and from all sorts of knobs and switches.

More importantly, though, this car had the regular habit of having at least one door fly open at almost every corner. Much fun!

It was late one night as we turned off Harrison Avenue onto 10th Street that I fell out of the back door onto the gravel of unpaved 10th Street. I was three years old!

After watching the taillights disappear onto Grace Avenue, I figured I should run after the family, because they sure didn't stop!

A mouthful of dirt and some serious skinned parts made my pursuit of the car a little tenuous, and I caught up with the car as my sister was finally able to blurt out the news that "Ernt fell out!!" "Ernt" was short for Ernest.

No serious damage was inflicted, but I'm pretty sure I thought we needed to get another car.

We traded that 1940 Chevy after the war for a 1941 or 42 two-door Chevrolet, in order, I suspect, to help the only son stay alive for a few more years!

I well remember when we lived in the Cove for a few months; I got in the car and pushed the clutch pedal down. The car rolled down a hill and hit the bushes between our house and our neighbors.

I couldn't see out as the car rolled, so I felt like I missed something. I do remember Daddy announcing that the emergency brake would have to be used as long as they had me around!

One memorable day, Daddy told me that he had done a considerable amount of business with the war effort and he wanted to share his good fortune by getting me something I really wanted.

Being a 2nd grader, but still really wanting a car, I told Daddy that I wanted a car, but an old car would be OK. He offered to go get a new pedal car, but I said no, I want a real car—one from the junkyard. It doesn't have to run—I can just sit in it and "drive."

When I came home the next afternoon, Daddy had gone to the junkyard and had picked up a steering wheel and shaft, an emergency brake lever, and a bucket seat from a junked truck.

With the flat side of an axe, he drove the steering shaft into the ground, put the seat in back of it, and buried the brake lever in the proper place.

Driving my first "real car"

I had my real car! I spent hours, weeks, "driving" my car to all sorts of places, in my mind at least! I was usually afraid of the dark outside, but my mother couldn't get me to leave that wonderful collection of junk. (I think Daddy got it for $5.00.) The seat got wet in the backyard, and the old wool upholstery smelled, but nobody had a real car. Sooo, at age seven, I was hooked!

We got a new 1947 Dodge when I was ten, and I was allowed to drive it back and forth in the driveway, including into the narrow carport. I never scratched it and the car was really easy to drive with Fluid Drive. It wouldn't stall or buck, and I had my own pillow to sit on.

They never took the key out of the car, and I learned how to earn trust during this time. Soon, I begged to be allowed to drive across Grace Avenue to the huge field where our neighbors had their cow tethered! About one-fourth of the city block was vacant, so I drove back and forth, day after day.

My Uncle Karl owned W & W Motors on Harrison Avenue, and soon I was driving in the new Dodges and Plymouths every evening for the night. Trip after trip, big trucks, new cars, no problems. Not a scratch!

The Bay Line Depot. 1948

About ten blocks away at the Bay Line Depot, boxcars would deliver four new cars each. My job was to ferry the new cars to the shop and run back for the next car. Not many preadolescents were allowed to drive dozens and dozens of new cars, and a driver's license was just a dream of the distant future!

We took the big wrecker to the Bay Line to help extricate the cars from the train, and soon I knew how to operate the wrecker's winch, but power steering was still unheard of!

They didn't know it but I would have run to Dothan just to get to drive. And I never thought twice about the risks the company took letting me drive, much less did I realize what I was learning about responsibility and trust! They slipped those in on me.

My own first car was a 1939 Chevrolet that I paid $100.00 for when I was sixteen. It was only fourteen years old then, but I thought it was ancient.

When Daddy said I could buy the car, I drove it home with no brakes and it made him so mad he took the keys. I explained that I needed to bring the car home to fix the brakes. He still took the keys! I traded my old Cushman to a mechanic who was going to fix the brakes. The scooter had cost $350.00 two years before. Boy, was I a cunning bargainer!

But that started my quest to learn about mechanical stuff, which continues to this day. Later, I did go to Transportation School in the Army and those guys paid me, taught me, fed me, and even saluted me to do my thing. There is a God!

And then I discovered tanks. Not water tanks, but M48A1, 50-ton Patton Main Battle Tanks! 810 hp, 12-cylinder engines with a 90mm gun that would shoot further than I could see! And they paid me to do that stuff!

Somewhere, while in high school, I got the notion that old cars are special. And old cars in the junkyard are all calling to me as I drive by, "Hey, over here!"

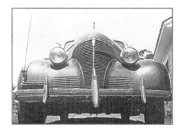

Front, back, and sideways: My 1939 Chevrolet Master Deluxe
with Bay High Tornado tag, parked at our house on Grace

As a youngster, I was always fascinated by junkyards and knew my way around every "wrecking yard" in the area. I sat in many nasty, musty, rusty, and smelly

My first business card

old cars and trucks. With just a little boost from my imagination, I could drive to any place on Earth!

Later, I started a business called "Resurrect A Wreck," and resurrected some old relics for their "new life back on the road."

When I get behind the wheel of a special vehicle out of my past, and it cranks up and runs and stops and turns, and the doors stay closed, I don't need a DVD or a TV to travel back to a special time. Euphoria.

A car is an extension of the owner and becomes essential to that person's idea of completeness.

Even if the "owner" is sitting in his backyard on a wet truck seat going "brmmmmm, brmmmm!" and his mother has to call him for supper ten times.

Thanks for the car, Daddy!

Panama City's Car Dealerships in the Days of Old

In the first fifty years of Bay County's history, many dealerships came and went. Almost a century old, Bay County has very few really old, continuously-owned local car stores. Cook Motor Company, the longest-lived dealership, began on Harrison Avenue and 4th Street, and their shop building extended behind the McKenzie house. Cook Ford moved north until it reached its current modern site on 15th Street.

Just down Harrison, on the property housing the Downtown Improvement Board was Pope-Harrison Star Motors. My grandmother made a prominent notation in her diary when they bought their new 1927 Star. Mr. Billy Pope was my uncle, and his partner later owned Harrison Motors, located at Beach Drive and 5th Street, across from the Paul Brent Studios. This was the predecessor of Kendrick-Rowell Oldsmobile. Just around the corner, near the Bay Line Depot on 6th street was Wilson-Sneed Hudson Motors. It was located in the Barq's Root Beer building.

Across 6th street, in the Amoco Transmission building was the Chrysler-Plymouth dealership. At some point, this building was also home to Kaiser-Fraser Automobiles, including the Henry-J!

Traveling south from 6th Street, on Jenks Avenue, directly across from the post office and in the shadow of the Dixie-Sherman Hotel, was Lloyd Motors, home of Cadillac-Pontiac. They had a gas pump on the Jenks Avenue side of their building, which also extended east to Grace Avenue, where the old Smith's Ladies Shop was located.

Just south on Grace Avenue was the James Packard Company. Mr. James resided in Panama City Beach, almost 50 years after the demise of Packard Motors.

As Grace Avenue ended on 4th Street, Harries Studebaker Company was situated in the triangle-shaped building, now belonging to Tonie's Dance Studio. The showroom was oddly-shaped and helped display all those Starlite coupes.

All alone on East 6th Street and Hamilton, next to Jimmy's Drive-In, was Rowell Motors, local Nash dealer. Airflytes and Ambassadors were all over the place, and the building is remarkably intact today. Former First United Methodist's associate pastor, the Reverend Albert Rowell, is the son of the Nash dealer.

Back on Harrison, Nelson Chevrolet-Buick, GMC, was located in the WMBB Television Station building. In 1955, Newt Tillman took over the Chevrolet dealership and moved to 15th and Florida Avenue in a new building across from the Ford dealership. Tommy Thomas Chevrolet evolved from Tillman Chevrolet. To many early Bay settlers, though, the "Chevrolet Place" was Nelson Chevrolet.

Farther north, at 7th and Harrison, was Padgett Motors, purveyor of Lincoln-Mercury products, which later moved to 15th Street. I remember looking at a new 1948 Lincoln Continental with power windows and a V-12, as I walked from grammar school across the street! I was ten years old!

Across from the bus station and Fowhand Furniture was W&W Motors, the Dodge and Plymouth dealership, owned by my uncle, Karl Wiselogel. He moved his business to East 6th Street in 1954, and became the Lincoln-Mercury dealer! This site is across from the First Methodist Church. Heath Motors was next to W&W, at the Harrison Avenue location. They sold Mercedes-Benz and International trucks. Ingram Motors succeeded Mr. Heath's dealership and moved to a new building, presently housing the Kia dealership on East 15th Street.

Last but not least was the Desoto-Plymouth dealer, Sala Motors. Mr. Bob Sala built his store in a Quonset hut in the 1000 block of Harrison, which is still being used. Mr. Sala gave me my first mechanic's job. He sold a fleet of 1956 Plymouths to the Panama City Police Department. This building became Bondy's Rambler before Fred Bondy moved to Dothan to run the Ford place.

Forever woven into my memories are the automobiles of my youth: those who sold them, those who drove them…those who fixed them…and those who loved them.

Where good things have been happening for over 52 years!

What to Do

My daddy, like his daddy, was a "bar" or "harbor pilot." licensed by the U.S. Coast Guard and the State of Florida. These legendary ship guiders had positions that were handed down to kinfolks for generations.

But, I wanted to be a doctor! Since I could remember, I was interested in medicine. Our family doctor and friend, W.C. Roberts, always encouraged me to aim for the soon-to-be-established University of Florida Medical School.

I was supposed to take all the math and science courses at Bay High, and Latin was also recommended. When I arrived at Bay High, at the age of fifteen (barely), the first shock I received was getting an F for the first period in biology. I loved biology! My problem was soon discovered to be simply an adolescent power struggle fueled by testosterone—and not all of it was mine!

Adjustments were made and I learned much. At the same time, after being highly recommended for Algebra II by my Algebra I teacher, I managed to tangle with my Algebra II teacher on the first day!

I showed her, though. I flunked Algebra II! I didn't need the course to go to college, I reasoned. However, my father enlightened me to the fact that I needed to go to summer school and pass Algebra II if I wanted "to live and do well…" So I went. And I made a C!

The other admonition I had, to further my chances of going to medical school, was taking Latin. The wonderful world of language and culture and fun in learning was opened to me by beloved Latin Teacher Miss Hord.

Lillie Hord (Brewton),
Bay High Latin teacher

57

She inspired me so much that I sought out any local source of Latin experiences, most notably one Miss Mamie Barrett, retired Bay High Latin teacher and neighbor of mine. Miss Mamie was old and blind and spent her days listening to all manner of recordings from the Florida Council for the Blind.

But I visited her and we talked about Latin! The blonde brat from down the alley would sit and conjugate verbs and decline nouns and identify the *ablatives* and *gerundives* and the *second declension*!!

And she talked to me about some local doctors she had taught who had struggled with their high school Latin! This encouraged me because I had some struggles of my own. Could I make the grade? I had sort of loused up my goals!

Off to the University of Florida and pre-med I went. Before classes even started, I knew that this was not the place for me. Even a spot in the Gator Band didn't help.

Clay Cogburn and I transferred to Florida State University at the end of the first semester, in January of 1956. We lived in West Hall on the top floor, and I imagined that I could see all the way to Panama City on a clear day! I was home!

Enrolled in the school of business, I took courses in accounting, management, and public relations, along with the liberal arts and Army ROTC. My least favorite subjects were those in my major! I wasn't a business prospect!

As an FSU student

Posted in the student center one day was a notice of a college-level, adult interest test for those uncertain of their real calling. So, I signed up, much to Cogburn's dismay.

The test said that I should be in a people-oriented field—social work, government, or education—and it indicated a propensity for sciences or social studies.

FSU grads, Clay Cogburn and me

I enrolled in Social Studies Education and loved it. A commission in the U.S. Army Reserve was coming after I graduated from FSU in the spring of 1959.

I planned to teach upon release from active duty, whenever that happened to be. But I loved Army life and was encouraged by my company commander to stay on active duty. More dilemmas and more decisions! What to do?

My old junior high principal probably gave me the best advice when he discouraged me from returning to my old school as a teacher. "Start fresh," he said.

A brand new school was being built in Lynn Haven, and I was offered a job teaching "8th grade everything."

"Wait! Even math and English grammar?" I asked Principal Bill Ross.

"Just study and stay a day ahead of them," he smiled and said.

The year passed quickly and I loved it. But the Army was still beckoning: "Come on back, Lt. Spiva." My class was full of spirited, wonderful, very special people. *They* set my final course. My first class. I would be a soldier on the weekends with the reserves

That first class in 1960 has gotten more special as the years have passed. We've had several reunions, including the one pictured below, and I've gotten to see firsthand just how my kids would do in this life. My most-prized memento from my schooldays is the plaque each student signed at one of their reunions. We stay in contact, talk on the phone, and get together, to this day. In fact, some of them have caught up with me, age-wise!!

Instead of my just riding off into the sunset, my first class is riding with me, just like it was back in Room 4.

I felt guided by fate, by my actions in past days, and by a few special people. And now it's so clear just *WHO* guided me, all along.

Reunion of first class at Mowat Junior High

I met my wife, Martha Costin, and found my calling at Mowat Junior High School in Lynn Haven. I am humbly thankful and so very fortunate. Martha and I both decided to pursue advanced degrees, she at Auburn and I at FSU. I went to visit her one summer weekend, and we ended up getting married that year. The Mowat folks were very good to us, and we were honored when the band performed a halftime show for us, and the cafeteria ladies baked a huge wedding cake—so everyone could share in our happiness. The whole school!

I graduated from FSU in 1966 with a degree in administration and social studies, in order to teach and/or lead a school. I served only one additional year at Mowat as assistant principal and was then sent to St. Andrew Elementary (SAES) as principal. The 300 students at St. Andrew were recovering from the previous year and the teacher walkout, which resulted in three different principals being assigned to *SAES* in that turbulent school year.

After two very different, quiet and wonderful years, Superintendent Thomas T. Todd summoned me and told me he wanted me to head up Rosenwald Junior High School, the former all-black high school, the subject of a federal class-action suit in 1970.

Martha's engagement picture

All fortunate organizations have a wise, experienced, and respected member, and Mary Alice King Herring filled that position at Rosenwald. She was a former science teacher and guidance counselor, and was my assistant principal when I arrived at Rosenwald.

She had been there *forever*: long enough to know many parents as students, and she had personally witnessed the many changes at Rosenwald. She was a godsend to us.

Mary Alice got sick and left us all too quickly, and in her memory, the School Board named our brand new science building the "Mary Alice King Herring Building." In a moving ceremony unveiling the memorial plaque, the picture below was taken, which happened to capture together some of the most important people in my career.

From left: Me, my minister, Brother "Si" Mathison, Superintendent Pete Holman, Abe Herring, and chairwoman of the board, Deane Bozeman.

Again, guided by Divine Providence, we assembled a staff of very young, aggressive, but low-ranking, new teachers who transformed the once-closed, vandalized, former high school into an accredited, innovative, sought-after place of learning: Rosenwald Junior High School.

I considered remaining at RJHS until retirement, and I enjoyed watching the school reach many objectives previously considered impossible. I even took my own kids, out-of-zone, past my old school to the new school, as my old principal once advised, to a much better school—over in Glenwood!

After eleven years, on my birthday in July, Superintendent Pete Holman asked me to go to Everitt Junior High so he could bring Everitt's principal, John May, to the District Office as assistant superintendent. A lateral move? What to do?

I didn't realize it, but moving to Everitt set the stage for me to experience the most satisfying days of my career. Providential Guidance!

At Everitt, I found a wonderful group of dedicated teachers and spirited students, plus a large corps of alumni who supported their school as adults. I learned of the "Eastside Connection" of community spirit found in Springfield, Parker, Callaway, Cedar Grove, Sandy Creek, and Tyndall,

Cheering the Bulldogs

"We care about the Eagles" became our motto, and very quickly the "Everitt years" were coming to a five-year, all too quick end.

Right from the beginning, students and teachers from Rutherford (RHS) would come down the street to Everitt and relate their daily experiences.

Rosenwald Band in the Christmas Parade

The two schools had a close relationship, sharing resources and enjoying close articulation—so necessary in education.

Everitt Principal

I remember being invited to attend a visit to RHS (Rutherford High School) by Governor Bob Graham, and I began to develop a very deep appreciation for all the wonderful things going on, unheralded though, at the school.

In the spring of my fifth year at EJHS (Everitt Junior High School), I was visited many afternoons by former Eagles, asking me to apply for the principal's job at RHS. The district was moving the 9th grade to the high school, and the principal at RHS was moving to the district office! What to do?

That bunch was organized! Every day when the high school dismissed, someone was *sent* to Everitt to try to convince me to put in for the principal's job. The pay was only $100.00 per month more at RHS, and it seemed that the hours would be longer (ha?), but something kept my interest up. Maybe it was that old Eastside thing, I thought. But it was from a much Higher Authority.

Coaching the Eagles from the sidelines

An 8th grader came in one day and said something like, "We're all going to RHS next year, so you've got to go with us!!!" All 600 of them, I thought!

Well, I *could* hire most of the EJHS teachers because the enrollment at RHS was going to jump and we *would* know most of the kids—and EJHS *would* become a middle school with 6th, 7th, and 8th grades.

OK. I applied and interviewed for the job. And it came to be! And I was excited. And the excitement never went away. Not even in retirement days.

I found so many new and wonderful people and programs. I felt that I would never master it all. There were some disappointments and tragic events, but these have faded into oblivion.

At long last, the district was going to build a new cafeteria at Rutherford, along with classrooms to help eliminate the need for a couple of dozen portable classrooms.

Promoting school spirit

But the work wouldn't be finished until the middle of the school year—and that meant no lunches, and no room, and much noise.

And it was wonderful: 2,500 students, a whole new grade, a new principal, no place to eat, nowhere to cook, and we loved when RAMPRIDE reared its head. That old feeling of community, of spirit and collegiality, and loyalty and more. I was determined that these kids deserved to be *first*, not *fourth*, especially when there are only three schools.

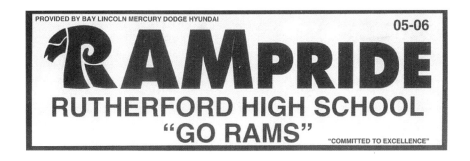

05-06

RAMPRIDE

RUTHERFORD HIGH SCHOOL
"GO RAMS"

"COMMITTED TO EXCELLENCE"

That first year, all the high schools met at the stadium for a "Just Say No Rally." Bay County Sheriff LaVelle Pitts came over to me and said, "The RAMS have **won** the rally and there was no plan for competition between schools. Your kids and teachers beat everybody today." I shall remember that day, forever.

That started a spark that grew and it still is growing. From athletics to activities and academics, Springfield Rutherford is a formidable entity! We did it. That elusive, slippery, human desire to belong and to succeed was nurtured and directed into becoming the underpinnings of a great school which met the needs of all sorts of students.

But I was **still** a soldier! As a reserve officer in the Army of the United States, I served in a local tank unit and later transferred to a civil affairs unit in Pensacola, drilling on weekends and at summer camp. This afforded me many leadership and travel opportunities.

Tank from local Army Reserve unit in Veteran's Day parade

65

Lt. Spiva on duty

I discovered that a career in the public schools interfaced well with a career in the Army. These experiences enhanced my ability to identify with the students and parents of the military families in my school and to form relationships with local military bases, especially Tyndall Air Force Base.

It became time to retire from the Army after 28 years from that day way back at FSU and my commissioning as a 2nd Lieutenant.

Now I could be the head RAM, full time!

"Springfield Rutherford." the Florida High School Activities Association's official title for RHS became known all over for excellence in so many venues.

When Florida Governor Lawton Chiles spent the day with us, he and Jillian Weise co-hosted the daily WRAM-TV program produced by our award-winning Communications Technology Academy and bonded with the RAMS. But what I remember is his remark about how great our school seemed to be to a casual visitor—even the governor!

Bill Clinton was the first sitting U.S. President to visit Bay County. WRAM TV reporters were given a press pass. After his speech, the crew gave him a Rutherford hat which he put on. That week the headlines of

Ernest with Governor Chiles on WRAM-TV

the student newspaper *Rampage* said, "Clinton enters Panama City as a President and leaves a RAM."

Rutherford petitioned and was selected to offer the International Baccalaureate (IB) program as part of the curriculum. IB teachers received specialized training in addition to their subject area certification to teach this prestigious world-wide program

From left, Glenda Fussell; Bill Fussell, first IB coordinator; and Karen Brown at the IB Senior Celebration

for academically - motivated students. Students from any Bay County school could apply to be accepted. All students were required to perform community service hours in addition to class assignments. Those who completed the program and passed the international examinations could receive the IB Diploma.

The director general, Roger Peel, came from Geneva, Switzerland to honor our first IB graduating class. He was impressed that we invited him to come four years before graduation, when we weren't really certain anyone would complete the rigorous program. A true leap of faith for teachers, students, parents, school board, superintendent, and the community!

With Fred Rozelle, presenting RAM Athletic Director, Clyde Mills (right), with the "Fred Rozelle Sportsman-ship Award."

The Florida High School Activities Association honored Commissioner Fred Rozelle by naming a Sportsmanship Award after him. It was given annually to one school in each size classification. The RAMS won the AAAAA Award twice in the first six years it was awarded. Clyde Mills was the Athletic Director.

The RAM football team saw a dramatic turnaround and went, literally, from last place to first place in one year! How?

Steve Hardin-Head
football coach

We lured Coach Steve Hardin away from Lincoln High School in Tallahassee with the promise that he would love our school and community.

And he promised to make us winners. Springfield Rutherford! A household name, now, thanks to Coach Hardin. His son, Blake, was a two-time All-American quarterback

who led the team to many victories. He used the same number 11 jersey that his father wore.

Rutherford coaches ready for practice

Blake Hardin-Quarterback

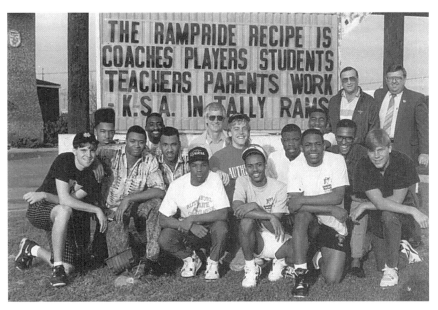

RAM basketball team at Smitty's Barbecue. Jack Smith was a big supporter of the Ram basketball team. He fed the team before home games and hired many of the players to work for him at the restaurant.

The Pride performing during half time at a RAM game

The Rutherford band, the Pride under band director Rodney Dassinger (Mr. D), holds the distinction of earning more superior ratings in state competition than any other of our Bay County schools. I hope Mr. Whitley was duly proud when I was allowed to conduct "Zampa Overture" in concert, played by the Pride.

ROTC cadets taking down the flag

Martha and me at a military ball

The Air Force Junior ROTC program always earned "The Honor Unit Award." the Air Force's highest rating for this organization.

The cadets performed many functions for the school, including raising and lowering the school flag every day and at special school activities.

Each year, in my Army dress uniform, I presented the Reserve Officers Association Award at their annual Military Ball and Change of Command ceremony.

The list of accolades is lengthy. But, what the entire grassroots level—stuff that every kid in school benefited from—that is probably our highest accomplishment.

Rutherford High School developed a business partnership with Tyndall Air Force Base. The school was also selected by State Education Commissioner Betty Castor to receive the first "Outstanding Business Partnership" award for their "Compact" with Tyndall Air Force Base. A delegation from the school went to Orlando to accept the award along with the Tyndall Base Commander.

We started the Academy Program and every student had to declare a major. Block scheduling and released time during the school day required commitment from teachers, parents, students, and the School Board. Everybody bought into the new initiatives.

When I would see a group of teachers meeting and planning, their new ideas were amazing. "The inmates are running the institution" was a term that made me profoundly proud! "Go RAMS!" had so many meanings.

Newsweek has recognized the top 300 schools in the nation for years, and more than once Springfield Rutherford was listed. Each year at Senior Recognition Day, students were presented millions of dollars in scholarships to Gulf Coast Community College, prestigious universities, and military academies.

Rutherford Rams Class of 1999 Graduation

Rutherford High School Graduation June 3, 1999

Rutherford High School
Panama City, Florida

Artist Judy Broome-Riviere

Now that it's over, I am only just beginning to understand how it all fits together. All those vast experiences, both good and not so good, were a part of a plan, which was propelled by so many folks, in so many places.

And it all comes back to Grace. God's Grace.

"10-4"

Photo: Courtesy of Panama City News Herald

Reflections on a Collector

By Beverly Fraser,
Rutherford Communications Technology Chair

You can learn a great deal about Ernest Spiva by looking in a cedar chest he keeps in his closet. You will find a uniform with his name embossed above the pocket. He wore that uniform 35 years ago after he left college at the end of his sophomore year, determined to become an auto mechanic. His early Army uniform rests in the chest also, along with a World War II ration book and numerous other mementos collected throughout his life.

His office at Rutherford was a more expansive version of the cedar chest. Under the glass cover on the top of his desk, were pictures from various stages of his life—Ernest as a ten-year-old, and then as a thirteen and fifteen-year-old, his children (both his own and those who have been his at school), and many others completed the picture. On top of the glass were various gadgets, pins, and loose photographs. Most of these items had been presented to him by former students and employees. The walls and bookcases completed the picture. Among the mementos were a picture of his high school band director, the stapler he bought during his first year of teaching, and a wooden puzzle made for him by an Everitt industrial arts student.

Ernest Spiva is a collector. He keeps things. But don't confuse this habit with hoarding or a sign of a stingy or packrat nature. He is a sentimental and thoughtful man. Each picture, each gadget, each article of clothing tells a story, just as he likes to do.

Retiring

Rutherford retirement dinner with Martha

The following tribute was given by the Spivas' son, Lee, on the occasion of his father's retirement from the Bay District Schools and Rutherford High School, in May 1999 when the "head RAM" stepped down.

Lee Spiva

"When I first read that my dad was really retiring and not just threatening, I didn't believe it either. As the reality of it set in, though, I began to think about the changes that were going to take place, both in his life and in mine. All my life, my dad has been a school principal, and a damned good one. I can't tell you how proud I am when I meet his former, current, or even future students and faculty who, without even one exception, tell me how wonderful my dad is. I know, like the rest of my family, because we are the luckiest ones. Imagine, if you will, getting those wonderful, hour-long lectures or the ever memorable "Army days" tales not just once a week or so but every day! Of course, being a good principal involves knowing how to simultaneously discipline and motivate. I'm sure my dad got plenty of practice in both of those areas before he ever got to school, thanks to the whole family (especially my mother). And now, we get him back full-time!

"When I was first asked to say a few words at this shindig, I had no idea what to say. Wonderful guy? Sure. Great sense of humor? Of course! Generous allowance? Well, maybe. We won't go there… Let's face it: all those who know my dad see that he simply gives it his all, night and day, at home and at work—doesn't make any difference. So, how do you pick out the greatest thing to say about a great guy? Luckily, a big part of my job involves driving around town a lot, so I've had time to figure out what to say, though at first I didn't know where to begin. I rely very heavily on my CD player to prevent spontaneous road rage, and as I was soothing the savage beast with some nice melody, it occurred to me that I got that trait, among about two million others, from my dad.

"Some of my first and fondest memories are of our family going to Sand Hills on the weekends to camp, fish, or sometimes just to ride around in whatever 4-wheel-drive vehicle my dad owned that particular week. For a while, he decided that he didn't actually *have* to have a 4-wheel-drive all the time, so boy did we get a lot of exercise pushing, digging, and hollering for help on the CB.

"No matter what vehicle we did have, though, we always had one thing to keep us company, and that was *music*. If my dad drove a vehicle for more than about two hours at a time, you could bet that there would be a radio in it. Always on the cutting edge of technology, he would, of course, have the latest *8-track* tape player that money could buy.

Not too long ago, I was rummaging through some of the tractor trailer loads of junk I had brought from home, and I came upon this dusty old case. When I opened it up and smelled that peculiar "plasticky" smell, it was like stepping into a time machine. All these old tapes—*Tommy* by the Who; Peter, Paul, and Mary; Simon and Garfunkle; The Osmonds; and even *Jesus Christ Superstar*—not to mention the entire Florida State University song catalog, including "The Hymn to the Garnet and the Gold." Let's not forget the many battle tunes and marches of WWII, the dreaded "Zampa" (if you were in the band), as well as a good dose of gospel, and not just on Sundays!

"I suppose then, the most profound influence in my life has been the man and his music, no matter what kind. That is something that I will always be able to take with me, no matter where I am. Bluesman John Lee Hooker once wrote a song called "My Daddy Gave Me the Music." My daddy gave me the music, too. Some of you have heard an entire symphony, and others might have only heard a few bars. My daddy gave me the music, and in being your principal, your boss, or just your friend, he gave you the music, too."

Afterword

The lasting message of one man's conscience
By Tony Simmons

When Ernest Spiva was principal of Rutherford High School, back during the six years I was the education beat reporter for The News Herald, I could count on hearing from him at least a few times a week. I'd answer the phone and the first thing I'd hear was:

"This is your conscience speaking."

He didn't always agree with me, or with the subject of articles that I produced, but we were always above-board with each other. And we laughed a lot. Over time, I think he found that he could trust me and I learned that I could count on him — both for story ideas and to shoot straight when I turned difficult questions his way.

He retired in 1999, just as I was ending my run with the education beat and moving into other areas of reporting. I did the math one time: He was 27 when I was born and nearly 55 when our paths first converged.

That year, he sought a doctor's advice after he began having trouble climbing steps or getting up from a chair. Tests determined he had a rare auto-immune disease, Inclusion Body Myositis. There was no cure, just treatments for some of the symptoms, and a prognosis that included a long, slow decline in health, falls, breaks, and worse. (You can learn more about the condition at the Myositis Association website, Myositis.org.)

But Ernest wasn't content to go quietly. He kept to an exercise regimen and never used a wheelchair except for temporary periods after breaking a foot bone. He was in his 70s when grandchildren came along, and they brought new joy to his life.

I bumped into Ernest's wife, Martha, at a Books Alive conference at Gulf Coast State (then Community) College in early February 2007. She told me he was getting along well after a series of health complications in recent years, and that he'd be up for a visit. A couple of days later, my work phone rang and my conscience invited me over for a talk.

Because his illness made it difficult to climb stairs, Ernest had to give up a multi-level home he and Martha had built off Deer Point Lake as their retirement cottage. They moved into an old house in Parker and slowly renovated and converted it for walker access.

It was a sunny morning when I visited. We sat in the Florida room and looked down a gentle slope past a heritage oak that stood on the quiet shoreline of Long Point. Egrets and other shorebirds waded in the sparkling East Bay waters. On the distant side of the bay, jet fighters turned and glided over the tree line.

We discussed our various coronary problems, mutual friends we had made in cardio rehab, and the importance of positive thinking. We talked about local history, family, and pets. Ernest told me awful comedies of his camping misadventures, and how his illness had changed his everyday life.

He was working on a memoir of his younger years, he said. He wanted to call it "Growing Up On Grace," which was both a reference to the Panama City street where he lived as a child and a nod to the blessings that he had received in his life.

I found it telling that he looked to his blessings when so many others would have been trapped in sorrow over what they had lost.

I had the opportunity to read those stories a few years later, and I noticed that—while he enjoyed looking back and telling funny tales— Ernest never failed to encourage those around him to think about their futures. I think that's the takeaway he left me with, at least in this moment.

Ernest passed away the day after his 77th birthday, and so many of the people he encouraged and supported over the years gathered to pay respects and pay it forward, just as he did. A Facebook page "Remembering Ernest Spiva," was established, as well as a memorial scholarship through the Bay Education Foundation.

Ernest truly believed in paying it forward. That is, he told me how he was visited in the hospital by a heart surgery survivor who gave him hope and helped him understand what he was going through; as repayment, he was asked to pass the hope—and dare I say, the grace—to others.

"Now you have to go and visit two other people who have had this, and when they get better they're supposed to go visit two more, and so on," he said.

Did you hear that? That was your conscience speaking.

Tony Simmons is an author and longtime reporter/editor for the Panama City News Herald and PanamaCity.com. For more information about him, visit TonySimmons.info.

Martha and Ernest Spiva, with grandchildren, celebrating their 50th wedding anniversary

Martha, Ernest, their grandchildren and pet dog Scamp

Epilogue

After a joyous celebration of his life, Ernest was laid to rest with military honors in the historic Bay County Greenwood Cemetery in Panama City, Florida. Next to him in the SPIVA plot is his father Ernest and mother Florine, along with numerous ancestors. His sister Betty Sue, and her husband Dan, are in the adjoining KIMMEL plot.

His marker reads as follows:

ERNEST R. SPIVA, JR.
JULY 20, 1937
JULY 21, 2014

HE MET HIS MASTER FACE TO FACE
HIS LEGACY—LEADERSHIP, LAUGHTER
COMPASSION AND GRACE

In Conclusion

As a leader, Ernest Spiva, Jr. sought fervent knowledge of every idea and project birthed during his long career as an educational leader. He was determined and resolute in attaining so many positive goals. Ernest as a friend, was trustworthy, genuine, loving of laughter, and would never turn aside any need nor dismiss a dream sought by those who knew him.

He faced obstacles in the seas of educational reforms; he sailed peaceful currents as well as encountered tumultuous storms during his life-long career. People under his watch while he was at the helm, felt affirmed and valued as teachers, staff, and students.

We all remember him as the epitome of good leadership and grace. Ernest has not passed, he is just away. The currents of time still flow and changes still come with the tides of educational reform.

In conclusion, Ernest Spiva will never leave the hearts and memories of those who encountered him. His life will serve as a reminder of a leader who acted; and what he chose to do, he did with all his soul and might. He has earned these words concerning his earthly accomplishments: "Well done, my good and faithful servant."

Judy Broome-Riviere
Rutherford Art Teacher

Ernest Spiva, Jr.